Grandmother Time Again

Grandmother Time Again

ACTIVITIES ✦ GAMES ✦ STORIES FOR GRANDMOTHERS
NEAR AND FAR

Judy Gattis Smith

DIMENSIONS
FOR LIVING
NASHVILLE

GRANDMOTHER TIME AGAIN

Copyright © 1995 by Dimensions for Living

This book is printed on recycled, acid-free paper.

Library of Congress Cataloging-in-Publication Date

Smith, Judy Gattis, 1933–
    Grandmother time again : activities, games, stories for
grandmothers near and far / Judy Gattis Smith.
      p.   cm.
    ISBN 0-687-00802-6 (alk. paper)
    1. Christian education of children. 2. Grandparent and child. 3. Christian education—Home training.
4. Grandmothers—Religious life. 5. Bible games and puzzles. 6. Activity programs in Christian education. I. Title.
BV1475.2.S6343   1995
248.8'45—dc20
                                        95-33084

95 96 97 98 99 00 01 02 03 04—10 9 8 7 6 5 4 3 2 1

MANUFACTURED IN THE UNITED STATES OF AMERICA

To Pattie Mattozzi,
friend and inspiration

Contents

Grandmother Time Again

Introduction

She was a grandmother who had traveled ninety hours by train across Russia to attend a faith conference in Austria. With the iron curtain lifted, she was again free to meet with other Christians.

Her reason for coming was simply stated: "My daughter knows very few of our faith stories. My granddaughter knows none of them, and I am beginning to forget."

Her words reminded me again of the important role of grandparents in passing on the traditions and stories and visions of our faith. We are a link in the chain of generations. We are the ones with Bible stories echoing in our memories and resonating in our lives and imaginations. Will our grandchildren remember the stories? Can we share them before we too begin to forget?

Our gospel, our good news, is a story made up of many stories. Stories tell us who we are and to whom we belong. Will our grandchildren be shaped only by the stories from the mass media and the consumer marketplace? In the midst of ever-changing religious communities, can our faith provide a significant source of identity for our grandchildren?

These are the questions that propelled me to write this book—a book of Bible stories that tell us how to live our lives. These stories help us shape our perception and our response. They tell what we value and believe in. They state, "This is who we are." Our faith stories—generous, encouraging, caring stories—answer a child's most important questions. They give, in an imaginative way, a means of coming to terms with life. "Doing good" is just the way we do things—bravely and joyfully, and with meaning. Our stories tell us so. We are able to see the importance of values because we have stories about them.

Since our grandchildren sometimes perceive the Bible as antiquated and dull, I have tried to tell these glorious stories in as creative, varied, fun, and palatable a way as possible, while still remaining true to the intent. Then I "grandmother tested" the stories. Children don't pretend to like things that bore them. An older grandchild said, in describing boredom, "That class was MEGO" (my eyes glazed over).

I seek to show the love that is conveyed in the personal telling of the story. Chapter headings pick up the virtue we are teaching. In "Importance of the Story," we seek background and understanding, and attempt to make the stories relevant to the lives of the children.

"Following Up the Story" suggests simple activities for you and your grandchild to do together in the child's room or some other quiet place: arts and crafts projects, or just talking together. Children love having a personal confidant, someone to whom they can tell their joys and sorrows, someone who will champion their cause and give them advice when the future looks bleak. This section seeks to cultivate that attitude.

In each chapter there is a section called "How Well Do You Know Your Grandchild?" Through these questions, you are invited to enter their world, ask them questions, know their friends and their fears, and discover what is important in their lives.

The section titled "Praise Words" reminds us of the importance of continually telling these children of our unconditional love. Faith begins very early. We want them to know that God, as Creator, loves all children and sees us as worthy. Children first begin forming an opinion of themselves by the way others speak to them. We hope that hearing us make positive statements will be a subtle urge for them to do the same.

In addition, there are bonus stories for those times when your grandchild begs, "Tell me another one."

And finally—we are a people who practice goodness because God is good. Our stories tell us so. We believe in the inherent power of these stories to give our grandchildren what is relevant and timely for their lives, now and into the future.

Someone has said, "Children are living messages to a time we will not see." We send our grandchildren into the future fortified with the stories of our faith.

There is no need to explain what our grandchildren should learn from these stories or to use cloudy theological terms. We, in simple trust, join the grandmother from Russia in telling our faith stories before we too forget. This is a book to have fun with as we go about the important task of planting deep spiritual roots. An anonymous author wrote:

> And Jesus said,
> "Who do you say I am?"
>   And they answered,
> "You are the eschatological
> manifestation of the ground
> of our being, the kergyma
> in which we found the
> ultimate meaning of our
> interpersonal relationship."
>   And Jesus said,
>   "What?"

Forget the theological explanations—tell me a story!

CHAPTER ONE

People Who Practice Goodness and Are Grateful

A Bible story to remind us is found in Luke 17:11-20, the story of the ten lepers. Read the story and then experience it with a "say-along."

A biblical say-along is like a line-out sing-along, except that words are used, rather than melody.

In the following say-along, grandmother says a line in strong rhythm and the child repeats each line, parroting the rhythm. Rhythm is tremendously important to children. Each line has four beats; beats two and four should be accented. Also, voice pitch should be varied, so that lines one and three are louder and higher than lines two and four.

Enjoy!

BASED ON LUKE 17:11-20

There were ten men, *[child repeats]*
So I've been told.
There were ten men—
Some young—some old.

These men were sick
As they could be.
These men were sick
With leprosy.

Jesus walked by.
These men did shout.
Jesus walked by—
"Please help us out."

He heard their cries
When they did call.
He heard their cries.
He hears us all.

He shouted back,
"Do as I tell,"
He shouted back,
"And you'll be well."

"Go to the priest,
That's my command.
Go to the priest,
And show your hand."

They understood
What Jesus meant.
They understood
His true intent.

And on their way
(The stories tell),
And on their way
They became well.

Their skin was healed.
There was no pain.
Their skin was healed
And smooth again.

They leaped and ran.
It felt so good.
They leaped and ran
Like others could.

But one came back,
And only one.
But one came back
When it was done.

To Jesus came,
To thank and praise.
To Jesus came,
His thanks to raise.

Where are the rest
Who were made well?
Where are the rest
With thanks to tell?

They did not come.
They all forgot.
There only came
One—from the lot.

The other nine,
They hurried on.
The other nine,
Now here—then gone.

There were no thanks,
No swift return.
There were no thanks,
They did not learn.

We too are blessed
(It does seem odd),
We too are blessed.
Do we thank God?

See "Bonus Stories" for another say-along story about gratitude: "The Woman with the Alabaster Jar."

Importance of the Story

When grandmothers gather, we hear a common complaint: "My grandchildren don't write thank-you notes. They don't acknowledge our gifts." Behind this grumbling is a deeper concern. We want our grandchildren to be happy, and it is difficult to be happy *and* ungrateful. In a world where children have so much, how can they be grateful for "one more thing"? And how do you teach children to be grateful for relationships and the gift of life itself?

Following Up the Story

1. ◆ Play a game with your grandchild, in which you both think of all the ways you can say "thank you" (letters, phone calls, smiles, hugs, words, etc.).
2. ◆ Keep a shoebox full of thank-you notes your grandchildren have written to you through the years. This becomes a cherished box of special letters.
3. ◆ Ask your grandchild to draw a picture showing where the other nine lepers went.
4. ◆ At appropriate times, give your grandchildren family heirlooms.
5. ◆ Challenge your grandchild to find five things to be thankful for every day.
6. ◆ For Out-of-Town Grandchildren: Send a self-addressed, stamped envelope and ask them to draw you a "thank-you" picture of all the things they are thankful for.
7. ◆ Say thank you yourself. Use words of gratitude often.
8. ◆ Create a birthday banner. Pass it around the family and hang it up on birthdays.
9. ◆ Make a rainbow. Place a small mirror in a shallow pan of water. Tilt the pan toward light until a rainbow shows on the ceiling. Recall God's promise through the rainbow to always be with us.
10. ◆ Be grateful for the world we live in. Take a walk with your grandchild, collecting and counting the trash you see along the way. (Be sure to take a trash bag with you.) If your community has a recycling program, separate trash from recyclables when you return home.
11. ◆ Teach ways to say thank you: merci (French); gracias (Spanish); danke (German); grazie (Italian).

HOW WELL DO YOU KNOW YOUR GRANDCHILD?

To think about: What gift from you does your grandchild cherish most?
Ask your grandchild: What is the most wonderful gift you have ever received?
What is the most wonderful gift you have ever given someone?
If you could keep only one thing that you own, what would you choose?
What is the very first thing you remember?
What is your favorite time of day?
Tell your grandchild about a special time in your life.
Tell your grandchild about a special gift you received as a child.
List the names of your grandchildren and make notes below:

_____

_____

_____

_____

_____

_____

_____

PRAISE WORDS

You are one of the most precious things God has given to me.
You are my treasure!
You make grandmothering a pleasure.
I like the way you say, "Thank you."

CHAPTER TWO

𝒫eople Who Practice Goodness and Are Brave

𝒜 Bible story to remind us is found in First Samuel 17, the story of David and Goliath. Read this story to your grandchild, then experience it with a cartoon POW story your grandchild creates.

A cartoon is a way to say something with words and pictures. Cartoons are fun because you don't need to be a great artist. A circle head, a stick body, and you are ready to go. Even very young children can create these. (Grandmothers can too!)

On the next two pages are cartoon panels with captions. Invite your grandchild to draw the story, and then tell you about it.

(David hears about Goliath.)

Make believe you don't see him.

(David volunteers to fight.)

Either he goes or I go.

(David chooses five stones.)

I don't know, I just feel lucky today.

(The whole nation rejoices.)

You'll never guess what I did today.

Cartoonists sometimes use "sound language." Here are some funny cartoon words for loud noises: FOOFOORAW! TZIMMES! SHELMOZZLE! BLAT! ROWDYDOW! and of course, BOOM! BANG! BLAST! CRASH! Add sound words to your cartoon. Use these or make up your own. The lettering used for the words can get *wild!* Try balloon letters; tall skinny letters; brightly colored letters; words written on lightning bolts or inside funny doodle shapes.

For a different story about bravery, see "The Storm at Sea" in the Bonus Stories.

IMPORTANCE OF THE STORY

To our grandchildren, the world can seem overwhelming. With more and more people, and transportation and communication bringing the world closer, what can one person do? This story affirms that we still need heroes. We need people who act bravely against overwhelming odds. This story gives children assurance that, with God's help, every Goliath can be overcome. Stories with a biblical foundation can affirm our need for bravery today. Our language is full of impact statements: "It hit me"; "It suddenly struck me." We seek the same impact in these drawing experiences. You might point out that Goliath relied on his size and strength alone, while David used his wits and skill with simple, natural objects.

FOLLOWING UP THE STORY

1. ◆ Watch cartoons on TV with your grandchild. Talk about them. Share your favorite TV programs.
2. ◆ Have your grandchild draw cartoons on large sheets of craft paper, then use them for wrapping paper.
3. ◆ Look at advertisements and displays at fast-food stores for POW attention-getters.
4. ◆ Watch a biblical video with your grandchild. Be aware that the Bible stories on video have a special way of communicating. Many children's biblical videos turn the Bible into animated cartoons. This makes the Bible "a frantic, busy, silly entertainment. It is not the great Story. It is only trivial and cute," according to Jerome Berryman in *Beginning the Journey* (Dept. of Education, U.S. Catholic Conference, 1994, p. 64).
5. ◆ Families have folk-type sayings that they repeat. Recall and make a fold-out motto of your family sayings. For example, "All things are possible with God," "Where there's a will, there's a way," or "No pain, no gain."
6. ◆ Tell a story, "Once when I was little," and add a story of bravery from your family history.

7. ◆ With your grandchild, write a letter to your local newspaper, praising an act of bravery.

8. ◆ Help your grandchild memorize Psalm 46:1-2*a*: "God is our refuge and strength, a very present help in trouble. Therefore we will not fear."

HOW WELL DO YOU KNOW YOUR GRANDCHILD?

Do you know your grandchild's hero?

Do you know his or her biggest fear?

Say, "Tell me about a time when you were lost."

Ask: When were you really brave?

How does your grandchild react to children who are older and bigger?

What would your grandchild do if an older child were doing something wrong?

What are some things your grandchild would always stand up for?

PRAISE WORDS

You can make a difference.

You never give up.

It's great that you are not afraid to take a risk.

CHAPTER THREE

People Who Practice Goodness and Are Faithful

A Bible story to remind us is found in Exodus 14:1–15:21. Read from the Bible or a Bible storybook about the Israelites crossing the Red Sea. Then experience the story with a "call and response."

Explain to your grandchild that you will say a line, and the child will respond, "Yes, Ma'am." Then together, act out the motions at the end of each verse. Motions are suggested by the response.

MOSES PARTS THE RED SEA

Imagine that you were a child in the days of Moses. You and your parents and the other Israelites were hurrying out of Egypt, overcoming your fear through faith, in the face of danger.

Call: Did you see Moses strike the Red Sea?
Response: Yes, Ma'am.
Call: Did you see Moses strike the Red Sea?
Response: Yes, Ma'am.
Call: How did he do it?
Response: *(child holds imaginary staff, strikes up and down)* Thump! Thump! Thump! Thump!

Call: Did you see the waters part?
Response: Yes, Ma'am.
Call: Did you see the waters part?
Response: Yes, Ma'am.
Call: How did they do it?
Response: *(child holds back of hands together and moves them apart, out and back)* Swish! Swish! Swish! Swish!

Call: Were you afraid of the towering waves?
Response: Yes, Ma'am.
Call: Were you afraid of the towering waves?
Response: Yes, Ma'am.
Call: What did you do?
Response: *(shakes all over)* Tremble! Tremble! Tremble!

Call: Did you see your parents trusting God?
Response: Yes, Ma'am.
Call: Did you see your parents trusting God?
Response: Yes, Ma'am.
Call: What did they say?
Response: *(pump fists forward)* Right on! Right on!

Call: Did you follow your parents across the dry sea?
Response: Yes, Ma'am.
Call: Did you follow your parents across the dry sea?
Response: Yes, Ma'am.
Call: How did you go?
Response: *(hands move up and down, quickly slapping thighs)* Run! Run! Run! Run!

Call: Did the Egyptian soldiers come?
Response: Yes, Ma'am.
Call: Did the Egyptian soldiers come?
Response: Yes, Ma'am.
Call: How did they come?
Response: *(march in place)* Thromp! Thromp! Thromp! Thromp!

Call: Did the waters roll back over them?
Response: Yes, Ma'am.
Call: Did the waters roll back over them?
Response: Yes, Ma'am.
Call: How did it sound?
Response: *(big circular arm movements)* Whoosh! Whoosh! Whoosh! Whoosh!

Call: Did you dance for joy because you were free?
Response: Yes, Ma'am.
Call: Did you dance for joy because you were free?
Response: Yes, Ma'am.
Call: How did you dance?
Response: *(turn in circles, hands overhead)* Twirl! Twirl! Twirl! Twirl!

See "Bonus Stories" for another call-and-response story: "Jonah."

IMPORTANCE OF THE STORY

Following God, doing what we think is right when we don't want to, is not an easy lesson to teach children. God understands that people are not perfect. Sometimes fear prevents us from doing what we know we should do. When we talk about what our ancestors in the faith did, or did not do, we are recalling our own actual past and, at the same time, describing our need for an eternal Parent who plays the role of guide and authority. The stories touch our need for depth and substance in the way we imagine our experiences. All of us can remember occasions when we were immobilized by choices, impotent in the presence of opportunity because we were indecisive. We needed guidance. Our biblical stories give us examples of faith—something we can draw on in difficult situations.

FOLLOWING UP THE STORY

1. ◆ With your grandchild, make a prayer-chain bracelet or necklace. Cut seven strips of colored construction paper. On each strip, print one or two words from a prayer: "Help me always do what is right." Loop the strips together with tape for your grandchild to wear or hang in his room.

    Send the already printed strips in an envelope to an out-of-town grandchild. Instruct the child how to put it together in the correct order.

2. ◆ All over the world, children draw mandalas. Basically, a mandala is a circle or round shape of any kind, divided by two crossed lines, like a pie cut into four equal pieces. Wide driveways and smooth sidewalks are ideal places for drawing mandalas with colored chalk. Invite your grandchild to illustrate this Bible story with a mandala.

3. ◆ Teach your grandchild the Bunny Hop. Instruct the child (or children) to line up behind you with a hand on your shoulder or (if more than one child, on the shoulder of the child in front of them). Show these steps: Right foot to the side, touch heel to floor, then toe. Left foot to the side, touch heel, then toe to floor. Take three hops forward. Repeat these movements. If possible, listen to the hymn "Lord of the Dance" and do the bunny hop all around the room in rhythm to the music.

4. ◆ Find a large stone in your yard or nearby. With your grandchild, read First Samuel 7:12: "Then Samuel took a stone and set it up between Mizpah and Jeshanah, and named it Ebenezer, for he said, 'Thus far the LORD has helped us.' " Share the story. With chalk write "Ebenezer" and your grandchild's name on the stone.

HOW WELL DO YOU KNOW YOUR GRANDCHILD?

Ask your grandchild: What was the hardest thing you ever had to do?
Was there ever anything you were afraid to do, but did it anyway because you knew it was right?
What is the saddest thing that has ever happened to you?

What is the best thing that has ever happened to you?
What kind of stories do you like best?

Talk to your grandchild about keeping promises. Do you remember that your grandchildren are their own persons, and they may do things differently from the way you do them?

PRAISE WORDS

You did that just exactly right.
I can always count on you.
Way to go!

CHAPTER FOUR

People Who Practice Goodness and Are Accepted

 Bible story that reminds us is Luke 10:38-42, the story of Mary and Martha. Experience this story with an echo-pantomime. An echo-pantomime tells a story without words, using facial expressions and movements of the body. Grandmother tells the story with words and actions; grandchildren repeat the actions.

MARY AND MARTHA

I am a friend of Jesus, and my name is Mary.
(stand straight)
One day I awoke very early
(stretch)
and wondered why I felt so happy that day.
(hands out in wonderment)
Then I remembered that Jesus was coming to my house today.
(big smile, skip around, hum a happy tune)
I began to dress.
(pantomime action)
My sister Martha was already up and working.
She was sweeping the floor
(pantomime)
and washing the dishes
(pantomime)

and cooking the dinner.
(pantomime)
She called for me to come and help.
(beckon with a finger)
I did, but first I stopped to look out the window to see if I could see Jesus coming.
(shade face with hand and look into distance)
I began to help knead the bread.
(pantomime)
But I kept stopping to see if Jesus was coming.
(look again)
Martha had to do the bread over.
(shake head sadly)
I began to help arrange the flowers.
(pantomime)
But I kept looking out the window, and Martha had to do the flowers over.
(sadly shake head)
At last Jesus arrived, and I was so glad to see him.
(jump up and down with joy)
What wonderful things he had to tell!
But Martha continued to sweep
(pantomime)
and wash
(pantomime)
and cook
(pantomime)
and call for me to help.
(beckon with finger and frown)

Now it was time to set the table.
(beckon frantically and frown more)
Now things were bubbling in the oven.
(beckon more frantically and frown more and more)
I was so busy listening to Jesus, I didn't notice.
(sweet smile, hands together calmly)
Finally Martha lost her patience.
(throw up hands in desperation)
She began to fuss.
(shake finger accusingly)
I hung my head in shame.
(hang head)
But Jesus said, "Stop!"
(palm out in stop position)
He thanked Martha for all that she did.
(count off many things on fingers)
But Jesus knew how much I loved being with him, and he said that was best of all.
(smile, nod head "yes")

IMPORTANCE OF THE STORY

So many things in our society today send this message to our grandchildren: "You don't quite measure up." You don't wear the "right" shoes or clothes. You don't look like the stereotypes in magazines and on TV. You are not as athletic or as rich or as smart.

And our Gospel message shouts just the opposite: You *are* accepted, just the way you are.

Each child is special. The Bible tells us at least two reasons. One, we belong to God. Two, we are created by God. Read Psalm 100:3 and Genesis 1:2-7. Isn't it interesting to reflect on the differences in your own grandchildren? Can you find a special talent or grace or virtue in each child? This might be a special way you can help a grandchild feel good about himself or herself and become accepting of others who are different.

FOLLOWING UP THE STORY

1. ◆ Show these pictures to your grandchild. Talk about which child they think would make a best friend. Which would be best in sports? Who looks most like you? Which looks most like Mary? Martha?

   Say: "If I told you something special about each person, you might feel differently. Each person is special. There is no one exactly like you."

   Look at the pictures again. Imagine something special about each child.

2. ◆ Give your grandchild a strip of clay or modeling dough. Ask her to make people, as many different kinds as she can. Tell her to try to make each one special. Wonder with her about God, creating.

   Sing this song with your grandchild:

What a Fantastic Creation We Are

WORDS and MUSIC: James Ritchie
Copyright © 1984, 1987 by James Ritchie

3. ◆ When you talk to your grandchild look straight into her eyes. Give her all your attention.
4. ◆ Strive for ways you can make a step-grandchild feel accepted into your family. Listen carefully to his feelings.
5. ◆ Keep a special album. Add a picture of each grandchild every year. The child will be able to see the changes that have taken place each year. Let the grandchild(ren) write a caption under their picture.
6. ◆ Recall times you enjoyed being with your grandchild, doing nothing special, just being together.
7. ◆ Play a game. List as many good things about Martha as you can think of. Then list good things about Mary.

HOW WELL DO YOU KNOW YOUR GRANDCHILD?

For your grandchild to fill out:

One thing I do well is _____

_____

_____

I know a lot about _____

_____

_____

Ask:
How are you different from your sister? (or) Do you know sisters who are different?_____

_____

_____

Is your grandchild a positive or a negative person? _____

Which are you?_____

PRAISE WORDS

I'm very proud of you.
Only you could have (done/thought of) that.
You're special!

CHAPTER FIVE

*P*eople Who Practice Goodness and Are Joyful

 Bible story that reminds us is found in Exodus 15:20, the song of Miriam. Recall with your grandchild the story of the Israelites crossing the Red Sea (see chapter 3). What happened when they were safe on the other side?

Experience this with a rhythm-and-pump story. First, get the rhythm going by tapping a pencil on the table.

Second, add words.

Third, add body movements by practicing the basic rhythm-and-pump movement used in every verse, pumping arms up and down in rhythm, with fists closed, like we see football players doing immediately after making a touchdown. Follow diagram for other movements.

SONG OF MIRIAM

1. Horse and rider into the sea.
    (Lunge side to side.)

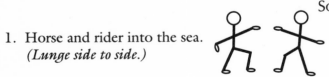

God has triumphed gloriously.
(Pump arms up and down.)

2. Water standing in a heap.
   (Arms side to side overhead).

Fear not, I will safely keep.
(Repeat pumping motion.)

3. Who is like the Lord our God?
   (Palms up, hands going side to side in a waist-high sweeping gesture)

I will save you with my rod.
(Repeat pumping motion.)

4. Let us praise God now—today!
   (Back to original lunge side to side.)

Let us praise God—hip-hip, hooray!
(Pump, then final leap up with feet apart.)

Keep the joy going by acting out Psalm 47:1:
"Clap your hands, all you peoples;
   shout to God with loud songs of joy."

With the next rhythm-and-pump song, sway from side to side, shifting your weight from one foot to the other. Follow the instructed actions, and do each line twice.

1. Clap your hands—doing do-wah *(clap! clap!)*

2. Stomp your feet—doing do-wah *(stomp! stomp!)*

3. Dance with joy—doing do-wah *(heel, toe [right]) (heel, toe [left])*

4. Shout it out—doing do-wah *(yee-ha!)*

5. All rejoice—doing do-wah *(jump, jump)*

6. Praise the Lord—doing do-wah *(shout Amen!)*

IMPORTANCE OF THE STORY

Our God is a God of joy. Here the grandchildren may be our teachers. Some occasions are so joyful that words cannot describe them. Watch your grandchildren jump and wiggle with joy. As we grow older, we appreciate the swift passage of time and, because of this, we can savor every enjoyable moment with our grandchildren. One of the most important gifts we can give our grandchildren is a happy memory. These happy moments can be imprinted in their memory with music and movement.

FOLLOWING UP THE STORY

1. ◆ Teach camp songs to your grandchildren. Bring the songs to life. Remember "Coming 'Round the Mountain"; "Bill Grogan's Goat"; "The Old Grey Mare"; "John Jacob Jingleheimer Schmidt"? Add your favorite.
2. ◆ Be silly with your grandchild. Make vitality more important than dignity. Children like funny sounds. Hold your nose and talk to them. To create a hollow sound, snap your cheek with your forefinger and thumb, with your mouth in the "O" shape.
3. ◆ Learn their favorite silly songs.
4. ◆ Memorize some "knock-knock" jokes to tell your grandchild.
5. ◆ Make music by humming into a kazoo. Begin with "Jesus Loves Me." Did you know that January 28 is National Kazoo Day?
6. ◆ Play musical games with your grandchildren: "Ring-Around-the-Rosy"; "Hokey Pokey"; "Here We Go 'Round the Mulberry Bush."
7. ◆ Children seem to find great joy in running quickly. Write a prayer with your grandchild, thanking God for all things that move swiftly. How many can you think of? For example: flying birds, blowing winds, fish in the stream, waterfalls, and running grandchildren.
8. ◆ Tell your grandchild how you played as a child. What games did you like? Who did you play with?
9. ◆ Sometimes children wiggle with joy. Ask, "What can you wiggle? Fingers? Feet? Toes? Arms? Shoulders? Neck? Body?" Put them all together for a total "Wiggle Wobble."
10. ◆ Send a calendar to an out-of-town grandchild with special family occasions marked in red (birthdays, etc.).

11. ◆ Remember to make ordinary, everyday experiences pleasant for your grandchild too.
12. ◆ Visit a zoo and tell the Christmas story while you're there.

HOW WELL DO YOU KNOW YOUR GRANDCHILD?

What makes your grandchild laugh?
What is her favorite game? Watch your grandchild at play.
What kind of music does your grandchild like best?
What kind of exercise does he like best?
What is your grandchild's favorite time of year?
What is your grandchild's favorite Bible verse?

PRAISE WORDS

Look at you!
Awesome!
You are so much fun!

CHAPTER SIX

*P*eople Who Practice Goodness and Trust

A Bible story that reminds us is found in Genesis 28:10-17, the story of Jacob's ladder. This story should be told only in whispers. It is a good story for bedtime, naptime, or quiet time. Darken the room. Remove all distracting noises. Whisper, so that children must listen carefully. (They like this!) Now begin the story:

Shut your eyes and listen carefully. We can hear better with our eyes closed, and I am only going to whisper this story. Listen. It is a story our people have told for hundreds of years.

To get ready for the story—with your eyes still closed—try to see the color blue. Can you see it? Feel the coolness of blue. Now try to form pictures in your mind. Blue is the sky. See it stretching higher and higher. Now, see a ladder reaching up, up to the sky. Can you see it? (pause). There is something on the ladder—going up and down—like many lights, soft and floating and white (pause). The lights are angels going up and down the ladder. Picture your angels.

Now you may open your eyes.

Our story is the story of Jacob's ladder. Many years ago, we had an ancestor named Jacob. Jacob had done a terrible thing, a thing so bad that it could only be whispered. He had cheated his own twin brother, Esau, out of the family blessing that belonged to him. Jacob had disguised himself and pretended to be Esau. Their father, Abraham, was very old and blind, and he gave the family blessing to Jacob instead of to Esau.

When Esau found out about it, he was mad! In fact, Esau was so mad that Jacob feared Esau would kill him.

And so Jacob ran away from home. He felt guilty and frightened and lonely. He went on and on—anxious to get away from his brother—looking over his shoulder. Was Esau close behind?

One evening after a long, tiring day of walking, Jacob lay down on the ground to sleep. For a headrest he used a large stone.

While Jacob slept, he had a wonderful dream. He saw a ladder set on the earth, a ladder that reached all the way to heaven. Angels were going up and down the ladder with the faintest of sounds—a whisper of wings . . . a muffle of steps . . . so very quiet. Listen—in your imagination—a little noiseless noise . . . a rustle . . . a breath . . . a sigh. Can you almost hear it? Angels close around, scarcely heard—soft, gentle—floating up and down the ladder. It is a mystery.

And at the top of the ladder stood God—a kind, loving, smiling God, reaching out welcoming arms. Wouldn't that be a wonderful dream? Remember the picture in your mind when you had your eyes closed? In Jacob's dream, God spoke.

God said, "Know that I am with you and will keep you wherever you go, and will bring you back to this land" (Gen. 28:15).

Suddenly, Jacob woke up. What a comfort it was to know that God was with him, even though he didn't deserve God's love.

And God promises us the same. God will always be with us and love us.

Remember the story. It is a story of our people. It is God's promise to us.

IMPORTANCE OF THE STORY

The spiritual imagination of a child is a very fragile, precious thing. Children live close to wonder. It is we adults who often feel the need to be rational and logical. We are the ones who feel uncomfortable with another way of knowing God. Do all that you can to cultivate your grandchildren's spiritual imaginations. They have much to teach us. Children seldom share their inner world of fantasy and perception with adults, because sympathetic, understanding adults are hard to find. You can be that kind of adult to your grandchild. Remember that faith is expressed in a sense of wonder—an appreciation of beauty. Share the wonder of the mystery. We do not know, but we do *believe*.

FOLLOWING UP THE STORY

1. ◆ Clear off a space on your kitchen counter and spray it with shaving cream. Using hands and fingers, your grandchild can create Jacob's ladder. Then, like a dream, it will slowly fade away. Be sure to use cheap, watery shaving cream. It works best.
2. ◆ Try wet watercolor painting. Soak drawing paper in a pan of water. Let excess water drip away. With watercolors, your grandchild can paint Jacob's ladder right onto the wet paper. The colors will blend together and blur (like a dream).
3. ◆ Give your grandchild a piece of art paper. With white glue, she can create Jacob's ladder and the surrounding angels. Then she sprinkles glitter onto the glue. Wait a few minutes, then shake excess glitter into newspaper and return it to the container.
4. ◆ Use white chalk to draw a picture of Jacob's ladder on black construction paper.

In all these methods, Grandmother provides the supplies and instructions, but allows the child to create.
A Grandmother Clue About Art Projects: If we fuss at the mess, we'll miss the fun.

5. ◆ Visit an art museum—just you and your grandchild. Look especially for pictures and statues of angels. (Remember that young children have short attention spans. If your grandchild grows tired, finish your visit another day.) If a museum is not accessible, look through art books together. Select pictures that express awe, beauty, and wonder. Do not impose your own ideas or interpretation on the pictures. Let them speak to the child.

Where else might you go to look at angels? Stained-glass windows in your church? Christian bookstores? Window displays at Christmas? Does someone you know have a collection of angels?

6. ◆ Save all your old Christmas cards and spend an afternoon going through them with your grandchild, looking for angels. Let the child cut them out and arrange them montage-style on a large sheet of paper, until you have a "multitude of heavenly hosts," or arrange them going up and down a ladder to heaven.
7. ◆ Start an angel collection for your grandchild. God's messengers are pictured in many ways. As you travel, look for unique angels to bring to your grandchild.

8. ◆ Carve designs on candles. Choose a pillar candle with color throughout. Soften the candle by heating for a few seconds on a paper towel in a microwave oven. With a plastic knife, your grandchild can carve an image from this Bible story onto the candle.

9. ◆ Soap also has a great potential for carving. During his nighttime bath, give your grandchild a bar of soap and a plastic knife. Failures won't go to waste, for they can always be used for washing!

HOW WELL DO YOU KNOW YOUR GRANDCHILD?

Ask your grandchild: "What is the best dream you ever had?"
Have you ever looked at the stars with your grandchild?
Can your grandchild make up a pleasant dream? (Remember—you can do anything you want in a dream!)
What secret can you whisper to your grandchild?
Together, try to imagine what the world will be like in one hundred years.
Does your grandchild play "pretend"? Who or what does she pretend to be?

PRAISE WORDS

I love you *(in a whisper)*.
What a great imagination you have!
You are wonderful—*wonder full*.

CHAPTER SEVEN

People Who Practice Goodness and Share

A Bible story that reminds us is found in John 6:1-14, the story of the boy with the loaves and fishes. Experience this with a "hear-what-happened-then" story. This story is sung, but you and your grandchild don't need to be professional singers to enjoy this story. A simple four-note melody intones a sentence in the story. This same sentence is repeated, with the same four-note melody, but pitched one note higher. Then for emphasis, the same sentence and melody is again repeated, stepping up one more note. For example:
Jesus on a hill (F-G-A-F-G); Jesus on a hill (G-A-Bb-G-A); Jesus on a hill (A-Bb-C-A-Bb).

Je - sus on a hill, Je - sus on a hill, Je - sus on a hill.

Then say the phrase, "Hear what happened then," as the notes descend to the beginning pitch (C-Bb-A-G-F).

Hear what hap - pened then

Now a new sentence begins, following the same pattern. That sentence is repeated two more times, each time on a rising pitch, and then the phrase, "Hear what happened then."

THE BOY WITH LOAVES AND FISHES

1. Jesus on a hill.
   Jesus on a hill.
   Jesus on a hill.
   Hear what happened then.

2. Five thousand people there.
   Five thousand people there.
   Five thousand people there.
   Hear what happened then.

3. All day long he preached.
   All day long he preached.
   All day long he preached.
   Hear what happened then.

4. Boy with a lunch.
   Boy with a lunch.
   Boy with a lunch.
   Hear what happened then.

5. Lunch was very small.
   Lunch was very small.
   Lunch was very small.
   Hear what happened then.

6. Jesus took the lunch.
   Jesus took the lunch.
   Jesus took the lunch.
   Hear what happened then.

7. Jesus blessed the food.
   Jesus blessed the food.
   Jesus blessed the food.
   Hear what happened then.

8. He gave food to all.
   He gave food to all.
   He gave food to all.
   Hear what happened then.

9. There was food enough.
   There was food enough.
   There was food enough.
   Hear what happened then.

10. It fed them every one.
    It fed them every one.
    It fed them every one.
    Hear what happened then.

11. A miracle from God.
    A miracle from God.
    A miracle from God.
    And they happen still.

See Bonus Stories for another hear-what-happened-then story, "The Storm at Sea."

Sometimes it is fun to find out if the children have understood a story by telling it wrong. Did your grandchildren understand your singing story? You might check like this:

Grandmother: Let's see if we understood the story. Jesus was in a house?
Children: No! On a hill.
Grandmother: Oh, yes, that's right. There were three people there?
Children: No! Five thousand people.
Grandmother: Oh, yes, that's right. Jesus was on a hillside preaching, and five thousand people were listening.
Children: Yes.
Grandmother: Everyone had brought their lunch?
Children: No! Only one little boy had brought his lunch.
Grandmother: Oh, I see. He ate his lunch when he got hungry.
Children: No! He gave his lunch to Jesus.
Grandmother: Oh, that's right. There was one little boy in the crowd, and when all the people began to get hungry, he gave his lunch to Jesus.
Children: Yes!
Grandmother: And Jesus ate the lunch.
Children: No! He shared it with all the people.
Grandmother: Oh, yes. How did he do that?

(Let your grandchildren finish telling the story to you.)

IMPORTANCE OF THE STORY

Every young child must learn to share—and it is not easy. Even we grandmothers still deal with this issue.

In this story, which is recorded six times in the four Gospels (more often than any other story), Jesus uses food to teach about sharing, and the central character of the story is a child. It teaches us that when we share, everyone is nourished.

FOLLOWING UP THE STORY

1. ◆ With your grandchild, think of as many "five and two" meals as you can. For example: five peanut butter crackers and two bananas; five pieces of cheese and two apples; five slices of beef jerky and two cherry tomatoes; five crackers and two sardines; five little doughnuts and two minipizzas. Eat a "five and two" meal together.
2. ◆ Begin collecting pennies in a jar with your grandchild. Get penny wrappers from your bank. Donate the pennies to a food bank that feeds hungry people.
3. ◆ Share familiar stories at mealtime. Make family stories familiar through repeated tellings.
4. ◆ Have fun imagining things to share. Help your grandchild make cards for special people. Write, "If I could, I would like to give you _____." Fill in the blank with your grandchild's ideas and mail them.
5. ◆ Draw a map of the kitchen when you were a child. What appliances were there? How is cooking different today? What did *your* grandmother cook?
6. ◆ With your grandchild, create a new candy. What would it taste like? How is the wrapper designed?
7. ◆ Have a special prayer you use when grandchildren come for a meal. Even the youngest can affirm this: "God is great! God is good! And we thank God for this food. Amen."
8. ◆ Invite your grandchild to draw a picture of everything he has eaten today.
9. ◆ Memorize Ecclesiastes 3:13: "It is God's gift that all should eat and drink and take pleasure in all their toil."
10. ◆ Visit an antique store with your grandchild. Look for old cooking utensils or toys like those you played with as a child. Share your childhood.
11. ◆ Always thank the cook.
12. ◆ Tell a story from your past about "The hungriest I have ever been."
13. ◆ Look in your Bible for other stories about Jesus and food (Matt. 9:10; 12:1; 26:20; Luke 10:38-42; 19:5; 24:13; John 2:1-11; 21:9).

HOW WELL DO YOU KNOW YOUR GRANDCHILD?

What is your grandchild's favorite food?
How would your grandchild complete this sentence: "If I had $10 to spend on food, I'd spend it on

——

——."

Ask your grandchild, "What is the most fun you have had when you gave something away?"
Ask, "What is the hungriest you have ever been?"
Would your grandchild prefer an ice-cream sandwich, a chocolate-chip cookie, or strawberry shortcake?

PRAISE WORDS

Wow!
Hooray for you!
I really like you.

CHAPTER EIGHT

People Who Practice Goodness and Are Loving

 Bible story that reminds us is found in Mark 2:1-13, the story of Jesus and the friends on the roof. This story is written with a rhyming word at the end of every fourth line. For fun, see if your grandchild can shout the rhyming word before you say it. Use a sing-song style of reading, emphasizing rhythmic qualities.

THE FRIENDS ON THE ROOF

1. The sick man lay upon the bed.
   His body ached, his spirit low,
   When suddenly four friends appeared
   And said, "Come on, let's _____ *go)."*

2. "We've heard that Jesus is in town.
   We're taking you right there."
   Each took a corner of his bed
   And lifted him in the _____ *(air).*

3. Then down the street the party marched.
   They knew that they were doing right.
   And the poor, sick man just bounced along
   And tried to hold on _____ *(tight).*

4. They reached the place where Jesus preached,
   But many crowded round.
   They could not bring their friend to him.
   They laid him on the _____*(ground).*

5. "What will we do? Jesus can't see.
   He won't know where we are.
   We were so sure that he could heal.
   We've traveled oh, so _____ *(far)."*

6. "We can't give up. We must have heart.
   Nothing can make us stop.
   We won't stay here. We won't give up.
   We'll take him to the _____ *(top)."*

7. The roof was flat. The stairs were there.
   They marched up on that day.
   To the top of the roof, the four friends went.
   On the bed, the sick man _____ *(lay).*

8. Another problem faced them now.
   They stood and looked around.
   They had gotten the sick man up.
   Now—how to get him _____ *(down).*

9. "Let's dig a hole right through the roof
   And push our sick friend through."
   The sick man looked in disbelief.
   What would these four friends _____ *(do)?*

10. Quickly they moved the earth
    away.
    Jesus was just below.
    "Hold on, good friend," they
    shouted with joy,
    "As down the hole you _____ (*go*)."

11. Before he knew what was going on,
    Before he uttered a word,
    The sick man was gliding down
    the hole,
    Like a bobbing, fluttering _____
    (*bird*).

12. He landed with a gentle thud
    Upon the waiting ground.
    The startled crowd, in disbelief,
    Looked puzzled, up, and _____
    (*down*).

13. But Jesus smiled at the poor, sick man.
    He looked on him with love.
    While the four friends peered, with
    anxious eyes,
    From the hole in the roof _____
    (*above*).

14. "Arise my friend," Jesus said.
    "There is no time to talk.
    Your sins are forgiven. Your pain is
    over.
    Pick up your bed and _____ (*walk*)."

15. "What did Jesus say to me,
    Speaking so clear and bold?"
    The sick man couldn't believe his ears,
    But he did as he was _____
    (*told*).

16. And sure enough, his legs could move.
    The crippled man arose.
    There was no pain. There was no hurt.
    He wiggled his fingers and _____
    (*toes*).

17. He walked and jumped and danced
    about
    Without a doubt or fear.
    And from four throats up on the
    roof,
    There rose a mighty _____ (*cheer*).

18. The bed on which he'd lain for years
    He carried without a bobble.
    His legs that were so stiff and hurt
    Walked strong, without a _____
    (*hobble*).

19. The crowd made way for him to pass,
    And some were celebrating.
    And there outside the crowded room,
    His four good friends were _____
    (*waiting*).

IMPORTANCE OF THE STORY

If our whole faith could be contained in one word, that word surely would be *love*. The simple statement "God is love" is basic, taproot, for the Christian life. We cannot *make* our grandchildren love, but we can nurture the natural love and trust with which children seem to be born. Is there any greater pleasure for a grandmother than to rock and hold a sleepy grandchild, just loving and receiving love from that child? By experiencing love in the immediate family, we hope that the child's love will extend to friends. This Bible story tells how friends love.

FOLLOWING UP THE STORY

1. ◆ Make or buy an autograph book for your grandchild. Have him collect the signatures of all his friends—one to a page. It will be fun in later years to look back and remember his friends. If there are school pictures to accompany the names, even better.
2. ◆ Be a friend to your grandchild by listening attentively. Show your interest without giving an opinion.
3. ◆ Create a picture called "Welcome to Grandmother's House." Using sheets of thin, soft paper, press the paper over a textured object and rub the side of unwrapped wax crayons back and forth until an image of the object appears. Your grandmother's house picture might include staircase treads, the bottom of your grandchild's sneaker, the concrete or stone walkway, the street number of the house, and so on. Overlap the images. It's fascinating to see objects appear and develop before your eyes.
4. ◆ On special occasions, give your grandchild her own Bible: a well-illustrated Bible storybook when she first learns to read; a *Young Reader's Bible* with notations when she is a little older; a King James Version of the psalms when she begins to love poetry or music; an NIV Student Bible in her preteen years. Consider other rites of passage when a Bible would be appropriate.

5. ◆ Teach your grandchild these two Scripture passages: From the Old Testament, Psalm 23; from the New Testament, John 3:16.
6. ◆ Invite your grandchild to make a list of everyone he knows. Learn the names of your grandchildren's friends.
7. ◆ Tell a story about a loving act from your family history: "Once your mother/father _____."
8. ◆ Challenge your grandchild to catch somebody doing a loving deed. You are helping your grandchild find the good in others.
9. ◆ Share with your grandchild how and when you met and married his grandfather.

How Well Do You Know Your Grandchild?

Who is your grandchild's best friend?
What does your grandchild like to do with friends?
Is it easy or hard for your grandchild to make friends?
Who are your grandchild's adult friends?
How many persons can you name who really love your grandchild?

PRAISE WORDS

You made my day!
Beautiful!
A hug from you—that's the best!

CHAPTER NINE

*P*eople Who Practice Goodness and Are Forgiving

A Bible story that reminds us is found in Genesis, chapters 37–50, the saga of Joseph and his brothers. A good Bible storybook about Joseph, appropriate to the age of your grandchild, would be a good way to teach the lesson of this story. Then share the fun with the following "good-or-bad?" story.

In a "good-or-bad?" story, Grandmother reads a paragraph, and the grandchild responds, "That's good" or "That's bad" each time Grandmother pauses.

GOOD OR BAD?

Jacob had twelve sons. Joseph was the eleventh son, and he was Jacob's favorite.
THAT'S GOOD!

No, that was bad, because the other brothers were very jealous of Joseph.
THAT'S BAD!

No, that's good, because then Jacob made Joseph a beautiful coat of many colors and sent the jealous brothers fifty miles away to Shechem, to pasture their sheep and cattle.
THAT'S GOOD!

No, that's bad, because Jacob then sent Joseph to see how his brothers were getting along, and Joseph wore his special coat.
THAT'S BAD!

No, that was good, because his brothers could see him coming across the hills and valleys. They could recognize the coat and know that he was not a stranger.

THAT'S GOOD!

No, that was bad, because as they saw him coming, they remembered their jealousy and decided to kill him.
THAT'S BAD!

No, that's good, because by the time he arrived, Reuben, the oldest brother, had convinced them to throw Joseph into a pit instead, so that later Reuben could rescue him.
THAT'S GOOD!

No, that's bad, because while Reuben was in another part of the field, the brothers sold Joseph to a company of traveling merchants.
THAT'S BAD!

No, that's good, because Joseph went to Egypt and eventually became a great ruler there.
THAT'S GOOD!

No, that's bad, because while he ruled, there was a great famine.
THAT'S BAD!

No, that's good, because Joseph had foreseen the famine and had laid up great storehouses full of food.
THAT'S GOOD!

No, that's bad, because his brothers and elderly father were also hit by the famine and had no food at all.
THAT'S BAD!

No, that's good, because the brothers were forced to go to Egypt to beg for food.
THAT'S GOOD!

No, that's bad, because the brothers did not recognize Joseph, and Joseph feared that they were still evil and would again try to harm him.
THAT'S BAD!

No, that's good, because the brothers had changed and were truly sorry for their previous evil deeds.
THAT'S GOOD!

No, that's bad, because Joseph now lived in Egypt, far away from his beloved father and brothers and could not share life with them.
THAT'S BAD!

No, that's good, because Joseph was so rich and powerful that he was able to bring his father, his brothers, and all their families to Egypt and give them good land there.
THAT'S GOOD!

No, that's bad, because many years later, their great-grandchildren were slaves to the Egyptian pharaohs—but that's another story.
THAT'S BAD!

No, that's good, because next time, I'll tell you that story—all about the escape from Egypt of Moses and the Israelites.
THAT'S GOOD!

Yes, it is, and Joseph said an interesting thing to his brothers: "I am your brother, Joseph, whom you sold into Egypt. And now do not be distressed, or angry with yourselves, because you sold me here; for God sent me before you to preserve life" (Gen. 45:4c-5).

We leave it to God to decide what is bad and what is good in our lives, and thank God that "all things work together for good for those who love God" (Rom. 8:28).

IMPORTANCE OF THE STORY

Often, children are the ones who teach us about forgiveness. Do you know a young child who holds a grudge? Children's anger may be swift, but so is their forgiveness. The Lord's Prayer says, "Forgive us . . . as we also have forgiven." Forgiveness is a gift of God. We must be open, like a child, to receive it. When we have wronged a grandchild, we can be quick to ask forgiveness. Perhaps you feel that your adult child or an older grandchild has wronged you. Why are you holding that person guilty? As we tell these marvelous Bible stories of forgiveness, we strive to model them in our own lives.

FOLLOWING UP THE STORY

1. ◆ Have your grandchild decorate white sheets or pillowcases, using fabric paint or markers. Make Joseph's coat of many colors.
2. ◆ With your grandchild, create an "I'm sorry" card to send to someone. Provide glitter, stickers, and precut construction-paper card forms.
3. ◆ Make Joseph's coat by cutting a circle for a head from a large brown grocery bag. Cut out two oval armholes, one on each of the narrow sides of the bag. Provide an assortment of decorating material.
4. ◆ Challenge your grandchild to count how many times she can say these words in a day: "Forgive me." "Excuse me." "Pardon me." Give a verbal reward or hug each time the words are used.
5. ◆ When your grandchild makes a mistake, be encouraging and help him learn from the experience.
6. ◆ Never scold your grandchild in front of others. It shows a lack of sensitivity and respect.

HOW WELL DO YOU KNOW YOUR GRANDCHILD?

Ask your grandchild, "Were you ever accused of doing something that you did not do?"
"Have you ever had anything stolen from you?"
How does your grandchild feel about an older or younger brother or sister?
Ask: "What are some things you need help doing?"

Ask your grandchild to finish these sentences:

I help people by _____.

When I feel bad, I _____.

PRAISE WORDS

You're on the right track!
Fantastic!
That's a neat idea.

CHAPTER TEN

People Who Practice Goodness and Are Hopeful

 Bible story that reminds us is found in Mark 9:2-13, the story of Jesus' transfiguration. This is a bedtime story to be told in a dark room that has a blank wall space. Give your grandchild a flashlight and instruct him to shine it on the wall at the appropriate time in the story. You also should have a flashlight.

JESUS' TRANSFIGURATION

It had been a long, hard climb up the mountain. The arms of the three fishermen were strong because they used them to row their boat, but their legs were not so strong.

Jesus had said, "Come with me," to Peter, James, and John, and together, they had climbed the rough slope of the great mountain near Caesarea, Philippi. Now at the mountaintop, the three disciples felt very weary. They collapsed on the comfortable ground, leaned against the sturdy boulders there, and nodded off to sleep. Jesus smiled at his weary companions, then moved slightly away from them to a place of prayer.

As he prayed, a great change came over Jesus. His face began to shine as bright as the sun. (*Instruct your grandchild to shine the flashlight on the blank wall.*) Jesus' clothes gleamed. Look closely into the flashlight beam. Can you almost see Jesus? (*Now turn on your flashlight and create another spot on the wall.*)

Other glowing presences were with Jesus. One seemed to be the great leader Moses, the man who had spent forty days alone with God on Mt. Sinai when he was leading the Israelites from Egypt to Canaan. One might have been Elijah, the ancient prophet who had heard God's voice on Mount Horeb, where Elijah had gone to escape the wrath of a wicked queen. (*Gently move the lights back and forth. Let the lights overlap and merge. Keep all movements gentle and flowing.*)

Just as all this was happening, the disciples awoke. How surprised they were to see Jesus clothed in such brightness, talking with Moses and Elijah. Can you imagine how they must have felt, seeing such a glorious scene? Then Moses and Elijah began to disappear. (*Turn off one light.*)

"Wait! Wait!" Peter cried. "We'll build three tabernacles here—one for Jesus, one for Moses, and one for Elijah." *(Turn off the other flashlight.)*

But while Peter spoke, a bright cloud descended upon the disciples. *(Shine your flashlight directly over your grandchild's head.)* The disciples were afraid. Then a voice spoke from the bright cloud and said, "This is my Son, the Beloved, listen to him!"

And then the cloud lifted. *(Turn off flashlight.)* Jesus went over and touched the disciples and said, "Don't be afraid." Now they saw Jesus only, for the bright light had gone, and the heavenly visitors also had disappeared.

The next day, they all came down from the mountain. Jesus told them to keep that wonderful scene a secret among themselves for a little while, and they did.

After telling the story, you might leave your grandchild alone in the darkened room to shine the flashlight on the ceiling and ponder the story.

IMPORTANCE OF THE STORY

What does it mean to hope? It means to live the words of the Lord's Prayer, "Your kingdom come. Your will be done, on earth as it is in heaven." What does God want the world to be like, and how can we help?

Every heart cries out for meaning. What a privilege we grandmothers have, to help our grandchildren satisfy this yearning. We give them our stories and help shape the daily events of their lives into a story. We affirm that the light has come into the world through Jesus, and is still coming through the events of their lives. We can help them discern the movement of God in their unfolding lives. For an instant, here and there, we can give them the gift of hope. This is the time appointed to us to do it.

FOLLOWING UP THE STORY

1. ◆ Ask, "What happened next?" after telling Bible stories. Make up a happy ending. Say, "Many stories have a happy ending" (this points to a redeemed world).
2. ◆ Greet your grandchildren with an "I'm-glad-to-see-you" face when they come for a visit.
3. ◆ If you like to garden, invite your grandchild to visit for several days. Every morning, go into your garden and ask your grandchild to tell you everything he sees there that was not there the day before.

4. ◆ Routine can be boring. Give your grandchild the Bible verse, "In my Father's house there are many dwelling places" (John 14:2) and invite her to draw a wonderful city with many houses. Color and decorate. How many colors can she add? How many designs?

5. ◆ Build sandcastles with your grandchild.

6. ◆ Tell the Christmas story. Relate how angels appeared to the shepherds, and use flashlights on the verse, "And the glory of the Lord shone around them" (Luke 2:9*b*).

7. ◆ Teach your grandchild the Lord's Prayer.

8. ◆ Supply soil, seeds, and containers, and let the grandchildren grow plants. Quote Thoreau: "Nature always lives in anticipation."

9. ◆ Teach your grandchild phrases of hope. Practice using them in sentences. Make bumper stickers with construction paper, then laminate them with clear Contact paper: "Glimmer of Hope"; "Never Say Die"; "The Glass Is Half Full"; "Look at the World Through Rose-colored Glasses"; "Look for the Silver Lining"; "Look on the Bright Side of Life."

10. ◆ Children love new words. Choose a "word-of-the-day." Listen for the word; use it in conversation: *trust, confidence, faith, promise, optimism, cheerfulness.*

11. ◆ Give your grandchildren core beliefs, so that they can cope with stress and trials. (See Rom. 8:28.)

HOW WELL DO YOU KNOW YOUR GRANDCHILD?

List stories from the Bible that your grandchild could tell without prompting.

What biblical verses or prayers can she repeat from memory?

Does your grandchild have the confidence that he can make a difference?

Is your grandchild usually happy?

Does she set goals and work systematically toward them?

Talk with your grandchild about his special gifts.

Ask your grandchild, "What is a favorite place you have been to or dreamed about visiting?"

If your grandchild were given one wish, do you know what that wish would be?

PRAISE WORDS

You are my beloved grandchild, in whom I am well pleased.
You are precious, and I pray for you.
Always remember that you are not alone.

BONUS STORIES

The Woman with the Alabaster Jar

(A SAY-ALONG STORY BASED ON LUKE 7:36-50. SEE P. 15 FOR INSTRUCTIONS.)

The day was late,
They went to dine.
The day was late,
The food was fine.

The house was nice
In which they ate.
The house was nice,
The service, great!

A proper meal,
A formal air,
But best of all,
Jesus was there.

Amid this pomp
A woman came.
Amid this pomp,
Mary, her name.

The guests were shocked!
Why was she here?
The guests were shocked!
She came so near.

For only men
Were welcome here.
For only men—
Should she appear?

And in her hand,
Clutched so intense,
A lovely jar
Of great expense.

She took the jar,
With perfume sweet,
And spread it all
On Jesus' feet.

The men all gasped!
How did she dare?
The men all gasped—
Perfume—so rare.

All wasted now,
So much expense.
All wasted now,
Had she no sense?

But Jesus smiled.
He understood.
But Jesus smiled.
Her act was good.

In thanks to him,
Her finest gift.
In thanks to him,
Her praises lift.

And what of us?
What would you do?
And what of us?
We're thankful, too.

In gratitude,
A thankful word.
In gratitude,
Is surely heard.

Jonah

(A CALL-AND-RESPONSE STORY. SEE P. 27 FOR INSTRUCTIONS.)

GOD TOLD JONAH TO GO TO THE WICKED CITY OF NINEVEH AND TELL THE PEOPLE THERE ABOUT GOD, BUT JONAH DIDN'T WANT TO GO.

Call: Did Jonah run away from God?
Response: Yes, Ma'am.
Call: Did Jonah run away from God?
Response: Yes, Ma'am.
Call: How did he go?
Response: *(run in place)* Rush! Rush! Rush! Rush!

Call: Did Jonah fall into the sea?
Response: Yes, Ma'am.
Call: Did Jonah fall into the sea?
Response: Yes, Ma'am.
Call: What did he do?
Response: *(make swimming motions)* Swim! Swim! Swim! Swim!

Call: Did a big fish come and swallow him?
Response: Yes, Ma'am.
Call: Did a big fish come and swallow him?
Response: Yes, Ma'am.
Call: What did he say?
Response: Glub! Glub! Glub! Glub!

Call: Was Jonah afraid inside the fish?
Response: Yes, Ma'am.
Call: Was Jonah afraid inside the fish?
Response: Yes, Ma'am.
Call: What did he do?
Response: *(cry like a baby)* Waah! Waah! Waah! Waah!

Call: Did he pray to God to help him out?
Response: Yes, Ma'am.
Call: Did he pray to God to help him out?
Response: Yes, Ma'am.
Call: What did he say?
Response: *(wave arms in air)* Help! Help! Help! Help!

Call: Did he promise to do as God asked?
Response: Yes, Ma'am.
Call: Did he promise to do as God asked?
Response: Yes, Ma'am.
Call: What did he say?
Response: *(nod head "yes")* I will! I will! I will! I will!

Call: Did the fish dump him on the shore?
Response: Yes, Ma'am.
Call: Did the fish dump him on the shore?
Response: Yes, Ma'am.
Call: What did he do?
Response: *(bounce up and down on chair)* Bump! Bump! Bump! Bump!

Call: Did Jonah do what he promised God?
Response: Yes, Ma'am.
Call: Did Jonah do what he promised God?
Response: Yes, Ma'am.
Call: What did he do?
Response: *(pound fist)* Preach! Preach! Preach! Preach!

Call: Did the people of Nineveh turn to God?
Response: Yes, Ma'am.
Call: Did the people of Nineveh turn to God?
Response: Yes, Ma'am.
Call: What did they say?
Response: Praise God! Praise God! Praise God! Praise God!

Call: Can you run away from God?
Response: No, Ma'am.
Call: Can you run away from God?
Response: No, Ma'am.
Call: What can you say when God calls you?
Response: I'll go! I'll go! I'll go! I'll go!

The Storm at Sea

(A HEAR-WHAT-HAPPENED-THEN STORY BASED ON MARK 4:35-41. SEE P. 53 FOR INSTRUCTIONS.)

Jesus in a boat.
Jesus in a boat.
Jesus in a boat.
Hear what happened then.

Wind began to blow.
Wind began to blow.
Wind began to blow.
Hear what happened then.

A fearful storm arose.
A fearful storm arose.
A fearful storm arose.
Hear what happened then.

The boat began to sink.
The boat began to sink.
The boat began to sink.
Hear what happened then.

Disciples were afraid.
Disciples were afraid.
Disciples were afraid.
Hear what happened then.

Jesus was asleep.
Jesus was asleep.
Jesus was asleep.
Hear what happened then.

Disciples cried for help.
Disciples cried for help.
Disciples cried for help.
Hear what happened then.

Jesus calmed the storm.
Jesus calmed the storm.
Jesus calmed the storm.
Hear what happened then.

He said, "Peace! Be still!"
He said, "Peace! Be still!"
He said, "Peace! Be still!"
Hear what happened then.

All arrived on shore.
All arrived on shore.
All arrived on shore.
And the story ends.

Jesus by the Sea of Galilee

(BASED ON MATTHEW 4:18-22; MARK 1:16-20; 13:1-2)

Instructions: Two grandchildren (or you and a grandchild) sit on the floor facing each other, soles of your feet together. Both extend both arms and hold hands with each other. Sway like a rocking boat, forward and back, as you chant.

Rock-y, Rock-y, Rock-y boat,
Rocking on the sea.
Rock-y, Rock-y, Rock-y boat,
Sea of Galilee.

Many of Jesus' stories were told along the shores of the beautiful Sea of Galilee. One day while walking by the sea, he saw two fishermen, and he called:

Rock-y, Rock-y, Rock-y boat,
Rocking on the sea.
Rock-y, Rock-y, Rock-y boat,
Come and follow me.

The two men did, and and became his very first disciples. Their names were Andrew and Peter.

Farther along the shore, Jesus saw two other fishermen in a boat, mending their torn nets. These men were brothers, James and John. Jesus called to them also:

Rock-y, Rock-y, Rock-y boat,
Rocking on the sea.
Rock-y, Rock-y, Rock-y boat,
Come and follow me.

They left their boat at once and went with Jesus, walking with him by the sea, helping him and learning more and more about the kingdom of God.

Once the crowd of people listening to Jesus became so large, pressing so close behind him, that Jesus went out into a boat so that everyone could see and hear him. Never had they heard such wonderful teaching before:

Rock-y, Rock-y, Rock-y boat,
Rocking on the sea.
Rock-y, Rock-y, Rock-y boat,
Come and follow me.

And many people followed him, because his words sounded new, just as if God were speaking to them.

It was by the seashore that some children came to Jesus. He took them in his arms to bless them and said, "Whoever does not receive the kingdom of God as a little child will never enter it" (Mark 10:15).

Jesus knew that little children would gladly believe him. He knew their little hearts were tender and quick to respond to his love.

Rock-y, Rock-y, Rock-y boat,
Rocking on the sea.
Rock-y, Rock-y, Rock-y boat,
Come and follow me.

The Shepherd King

(BASED ON 1 SAMUEL 16)

Instructions: This is a clapping story. As you read it aloud to your grandchildren, ask them to clap every time you say the words *King* and *Shepherd*. If you say these words together, the children should clap twice. It can be challenging, especially for young children, to remember not to clap at any other time. Read the story slowly at first. Then, for fun, you might like to read it faster and faster.

Long ago, there lived a man named Samuel. Samuel was a prophet who listened to God.

One day God said, "I am going to send you to Bethlehem to find a new King *(clap)* for Israel. There is a man in Bethlehem named Jesse who has eight sons who are Shepherds *(clap)*. One of them will be the new King *(clap)*—a Shepherd King" *(clap-clap)*.

A great feast was prepared, and the sons of Jesse came. First there was the oldest, Eliab, a Shepherd *(clap)*. He was tall and handsome. Samuel thought he would make a great King *(clap)*. But God said, "This is not the man. You want to choose him because of the way he looks. I care about the heart of my Shepherd King" *(clap-clap)*.

Then Jesse brought his other sons to Samuel. All of them were Shepherds *(clap)*. But Samuel shook his head. "God has chosen none of these to be King *(clap)*. Do you have another son? God is looking for a Shepherd King" *(clap-clap)*.

Jesse said, "I have one more son, but I did not bring him to the feast. He is my youngest son, and he is in the field, caring for my sheep."

Samuel told Jesse to send for the Shepherd *(clap)* boy at once, because God had chosen him to be King *(clap)*.

At last a rosy-cheeked, bright-eyed boy, dressed as a Shepherd *(clap)* arrived. The Lord said to Samuel, "This is the one I have chosen to be King" *(clap)*.

His name was David, the Shepherd King, *(clap-clap)* and he became the leader of Israel.

Palm Sunday

(BASED ON LUKE 19:28-38)

Instructions: As you tell this story, the children respond by snapping their fingers and saying, "Come, donkey, come."

It was a time of great excitement. Many people had come to the city of Jerusalem to celebrate Passover. On the morning of that same day, Jesus called two of his disciples to him.

Storyteller: I want you to go to the village of Bethany and find a donkey.

Response: *(snap fingers)* Come, donkey, come.

Storyteller: If the owner should question you, say, "The Lord has need of this donkey today."

Response: Come, donkey, come.

Storyteller: The disciples did as they were told. They found the donkey tied by the roadside.

Response: Come, donkey, come.

Storyteller: They told the owner the message that Jesus had sent.

Response: Come, donkey, come.

Storyteller: And the owner let them take the donkey to Jesus.

Response: Come, donkey, come.

Storyteller: Then the disciples spread their garments on the donkey's back, and Jesus sat on it.

Response: Come, donkey, come.

Storyteller: As Jesus approached Jerusalem, great crowds followed him.

Response: Come, donkey, come.

Storyteller: They waved palm branches and shouted, "Blessed is Jesus."

Response: Come, donkey, come.

Storyteller: Some people threw their palm branches in the road for him to ride over, and some threw down their coats.

Response: Come, donkey, come.

Storyteller: All along the roadway, the people stood rejoicing and praising God.

Response: Come, donkey, come.

Storyteller: Jesus rode through the gate and into the city.

Response: Come, donkey, come.

Storyteller: As he went by, the people shouted, "Hosanna."

Response: Come, donkey, come.

Storyteller: Some asked, "Who is this new King riding on a donkey?"

Response: Come, donkey, come.

Storyteller: And the multitude answered, "This is Jesus, the prophet of Nazareth of Galilee."

Response: Come, donkey, come.

Storyteller: Then Jesus got down and entered the temple, and the donkey that had carried a King went home.

Response: Come, donkey, come.